Bo

IN RECITAL®
with Christmas Favorites

ABOUT THE SERIES • A NOTE TO THE TEACHER

In Recital® with Christmas Favorites is devoted to wonderful Christmas repertoire. The fine composers and arrangers of this series have created engaging arrangements of timeless treasures, which have been carefully leveled to ensure success with this repertoire. We know that to motivate, the teacher must challenge the student with attainable goals. This series makes that possible while also providing a perfect holiday treat for your students. You will find favorites that are easy to sing along with, as well as recital-style arrangements of Christmas classics. You will also find some new Christmas gems. This series complements other FJH publications, and will help you plan student recital repertoire for holiday season recitals. The books include free downloadable recordings with complete performances as well as "play along" tracks designed to assist with recital preparation. Throughout this series you will find a charming history of each Christmas carol researched by Miriam Littell.

Use the downloadable recordings as a teaching and motivational tool. To learn how to download the free recordings and use them as a valuable practice aid, turn to inside back cover.

The editor wishes to thank the following people: Miriam Littell, for her superb research on the history of these Christmas carols; Kevin Olson and Robert Schultz; recording producer, Brian Balmages; production coordinators, Philip Groeber and Isabel Otero Bowen; and the publisher, Frank J. Hackinson, whose expertise and commitment to excellence makes books such as these possible.

THE
F·J·H
MUSIC
COMPANY
INC.
Frank J. Hackinson

Production: Frank J. Hackinson
Production Coordinators: Philip Groeber and Isabel Otero Bowen
Cover and Interior Art Concepts: Helen Marlais
Art Direction: Terpstra Design, San Francisco
Cover and Inside Illustrations: Kevin Hawkes
Engraving: Tempo Music Press, Inc.
Printer: Tempo Music Press, Inc.

ISBN-13: 978-1-56939-534-9

ORGANIZATION OF THE SERIES
IN RECITAL® WITH CHRISTMAS FAVORITES

T he series is carefully leveled into the following six categories: Early Elementary, Elementary, Late Elementary, Early Intermediate, Intermediate, and Late Intermediate. Each of the works has been selected for its artistic as well as pedagogical merit.

Book Four — Early Intermediate, reinforces the following concepts:

- ♩. ♪ rhythmic patterns are used, as well as sixteenth-note patterns.

- Students play pieces with common time signatures as well as simple compound meters.

- Students play pieces with more intricate finger crossovers.

- Students learn to play pieces with numerous changes of tempo, articulations, and moods.

- Major, minor, and diminished root-position chords and their inversions are reinforced, as well as subdominant and dominant chords.

- Students play hand-over-hand arpeggios and a glissando.

- Students play pieces in which one hand holds down notes while simultaneously playing moving notes.

- Students play octave scale passages and blocked octaves.

- Left-hand parts increase in intricacy with more involved accompanimental figures, or in some cases the left hand plays the melody while the right hand accompanies.

- Students play pieces with modulations from one key to another key.

- Hand positions expand to larger than a fifth.

- Pieces reinforce the following musical terms and symbols: *ritardando, diminuendo, fortissimo, pianissimo, allargando,* and *rallentando*.

- Keys of C major, G major, F major, D major, A minor, G minor, and E minor.

> *Angels We Have Heard on High,* and *The First Nowell* were arranged as equal-part duets.

TABLE OF CONTENTS

	Recital Category	Composer	Arranger	Page	Performance Track	Practice Track	Performance Ready Track
About the Carols	Miriam Littell Helen Marlais			4-5			
Angels from the Realms of Glory	Solo	M: Henry Thomas Smart W: James Montgomery	Kevin Costley	6-7	1	13	14
Deck the Halls	Solo	16th Century Welsh Carol	Melody Bober	8-10	2	15	16
Hark! The Herald Angels Sing	Solo	M: Felix Mendelssohn W: Charles Wesley	Kevin Costley	11-13	3	17	18
Angels We Have Heard on High	Equal Part Duet	Traditional French Carol	Robert Schultz	14-17	4	19	20
Ding Dong! Merrily on High	Solo	M: French Folk Melody W: George Ratcliffe Woodward	Melody Bober	18-21	5	21	22
The Coventry Carol	Solo	M: Ancient English Carol W: Attributed to Robert Croo	Timothy Brown	22-23	6	23	24
Silent Night (*Stille Nacht*)	Optional Duet	M: Franz Gruber W: Joseph Mohr	Robert Schultz	24-27	7	25	26
O Come, All Ye Faithful (*Adeste Fideles*)	Solo	M: John Francis Wade W: Translated by Frederick Oakeley	Edwin McLean	28-29	8	27	28
The First Nowell (*The First Noël*)	Equal Part Duet	Traditional English Carol	Timothy Brown	30-33	9	29	30
Christmas Travels	Solo	*II est né*: Old French Carol *Gesu Bambino*: Pietro Alessandro Yon W: Translated by Frederick Herman Martens *O Tannenbaum*: German Folk Song	Kevin Olson	34-37	10	31	32
What Child Is This (*Greensleeves*)	Solo	M: English Folk Song W: William Chatterton Dix	Melody Bober	38-40	11	33	34
Hallelujah Chorus from *The Messiah*	Solo	M & W: George Frideric Handel	Edwin McLean	41-43	12	35	36
About the Carols	Miriam Littell Helen Marlais			44-45			
About the Arrangers				46-47			
Using the Recordings	Helen Marlais			48			

Christmas carols were introduced into church services by St. Francis of Assisi 900 years ago in Italy!

Assisi, Italy

Angels from the Realms of Glory

The lyrics were written by hymn writer and journalist James Montgomery (1771-1854), in Sheffield, England and were published December 24th, 1816. His lyrical poetry may have been influenced by the eighteenth-century French carol, *Les Anges dans nos campagnes*, and it was sung to the tune of that carol for fifty years. In 1867, a blind English church musician named Henry Thomas Smart (1813-1879) composed a melody that paired well with Montgomery's lyrics.

Deck the Halls

This energetic song about caroling and merrymaking celebrates the happiness and cheerfulness of the season. The melody is around 500 years old! 300 years ago, the great master Wolfgang Amadeus Mozart (1756-1791) used the melody in a duet for piano and violin. The first known printing of the words was in New York in 1881.

Hark! The Herald Angels Sing

Charles Wesley (1707-1788) was an English clergyman, poet, and prolific hymn writer. He was the brother of John Wesley, the founder of Methodism. Wesley believed that Christian hymns should be joyous. Englishman William Hayman Cummings combined the lyrics of this carol with a melody by Felix Mendelssohn and that is how we know the carol today. The carol was published in 1856. The melody by Mendelssohn was first heard in 1840 as part of a choral work to commemorate the 400th anniversary of the printing press.

FJH1576

ABOUT THE CAROLS

Angels We Have Heard on High

This is a traditional French carol, probably created 300 years ago. Its authorship is anonymous, but the use of the Latin "Gloria in excelsis Deo" ("Glory to God in the highest") suggests creation by musicians affiliated with the church. The carol was first published in France in 1855.

Ding Dong! Merrily on High

The music to this lovely song evoking the sounds of angels singing and bells ringing, is an old French folk melody, probably created 500 years ago. It was first published in a landmark 1588 treatise on ballet dancing, so we know it was considered a dance tune. The lyrics were written by Englishman George Ratcliffe Woodward (1848-1934).

The Coventry Carol

The mournful lyrics of this song from the 1500s were written for the Pageant of the Shearmen and Tailors in Coventry, England. The pageant was a play based on biblical stories. The oldest known text of the lyrics was written in 1534. The oldest known printing of the music is dated 1591. This lovely and sensitive carol is one of a very few that tells of an unpleasant aspect of the Christmas story. The song is about the danger to young children from King Herod at the time of Christ's birth.

Silent Night (*Stille Nacht*)

This most beloved of all German carols was first performed in a little church in the beautiful Tyrol region of lakes and mountains on the border of Austria and Bavaria, in 1818. On Christmas Eve, church organist Franz Gruber found his organ out of order. He and the assistant priest, Joseph Mohr, quickly composed lyrics and an original melody for two voices and a choir with guitar accompaniment for the service. The song was first published in 1838, and by 1955 it was the most recorded song of all time.

Angels from the Realms of Glory

Henry Thomas Smart   arr. Kevin Costley

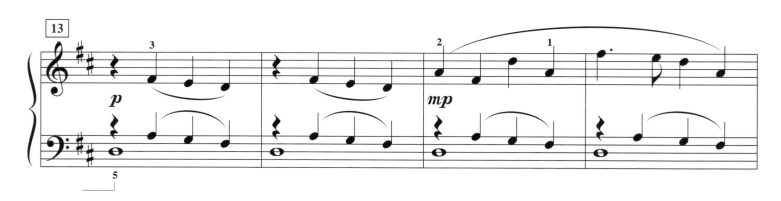

FJH1576

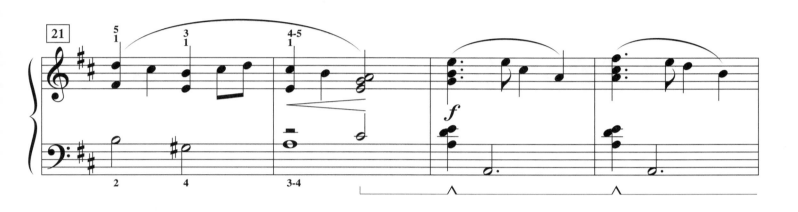

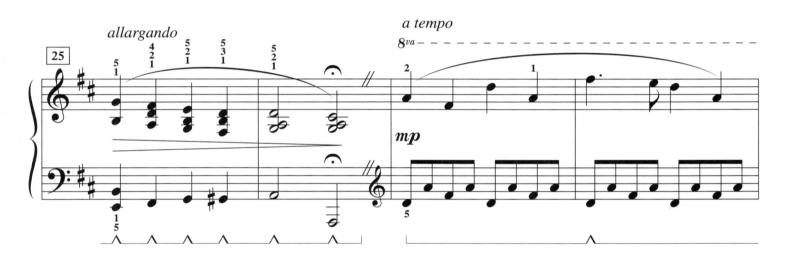

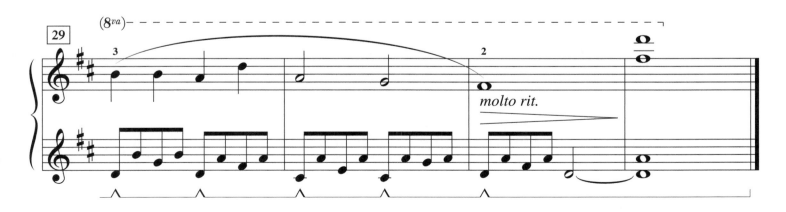

Deck the Halls

16th Century Welsh Carol   arr. Melody Bober

FJH1576

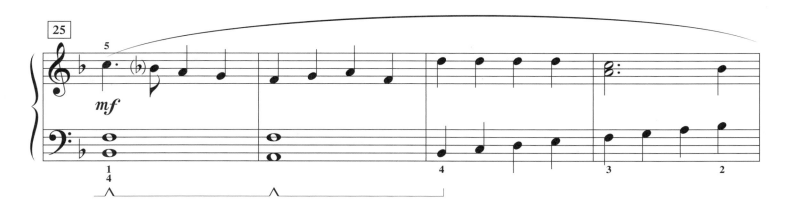

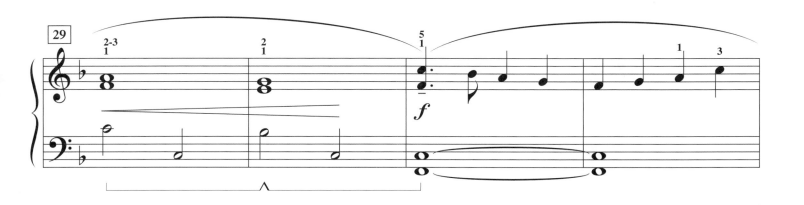

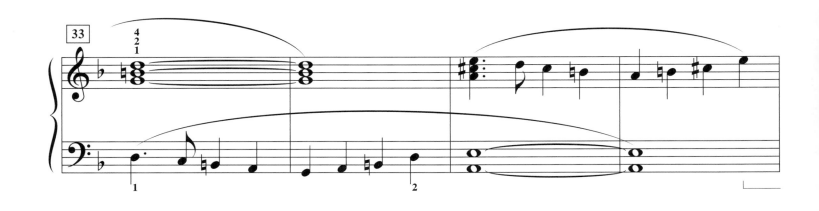

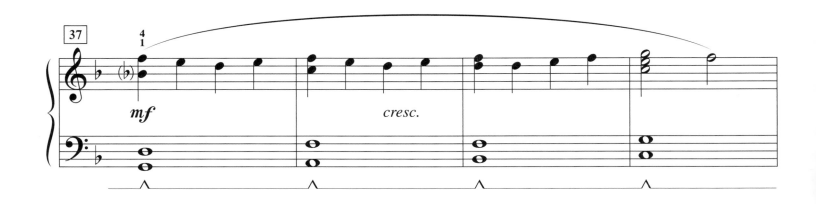

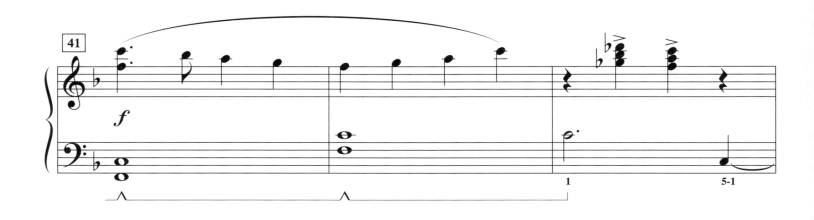

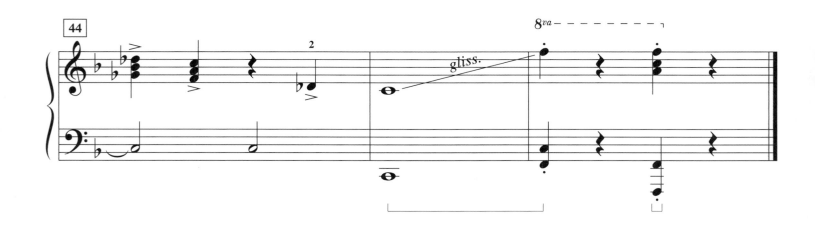

Hark! The Herald Angels Sing

Felix Mendelssohn   arr. Kevin Costley

With conviction

Angels We Have Heard on High
Secondo

Traditional French Carol   arr. Robert Schultz

FJH1576

Angels We Have Heard on High

Primo

Traditional French Carol   arr. Robert Schultz

Secondo

Primo

Ding Dong! Merrily on High

French Folk Melody   arr. Melody Bober

FJH1576

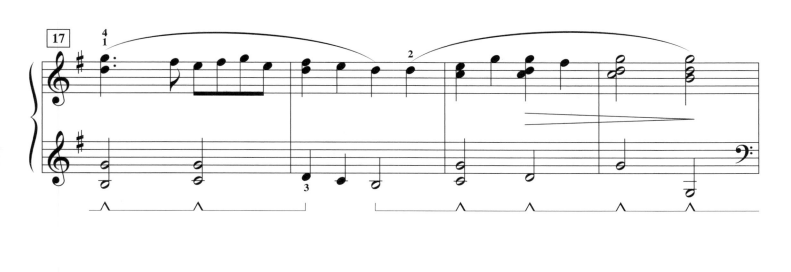

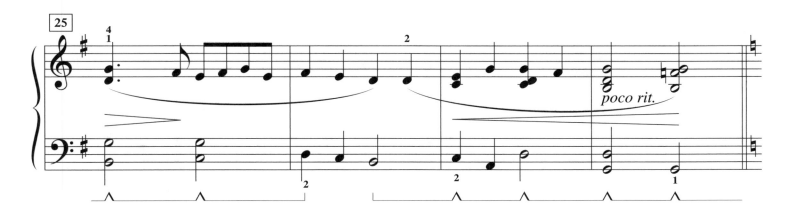

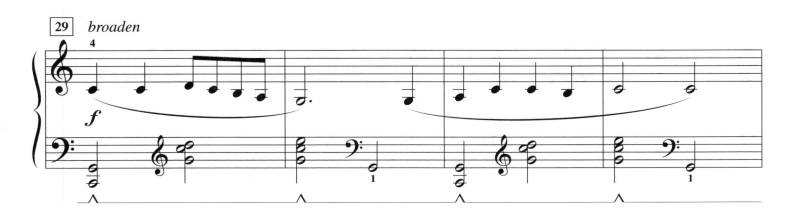

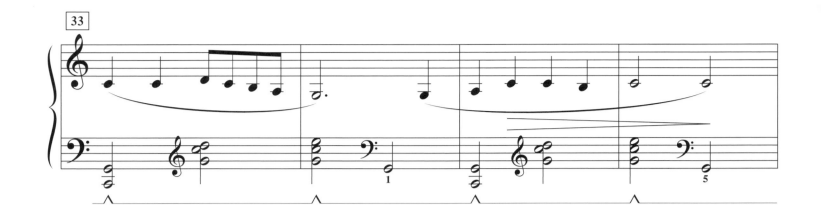

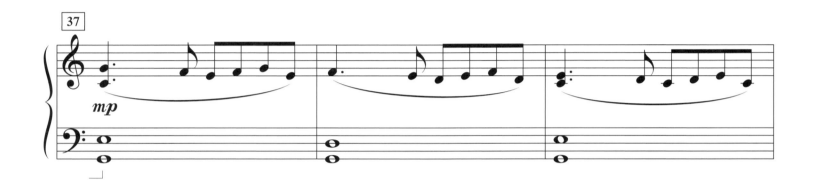

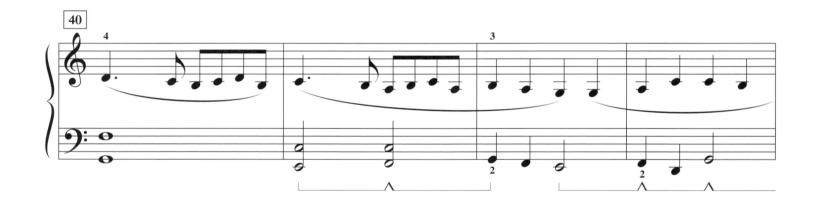

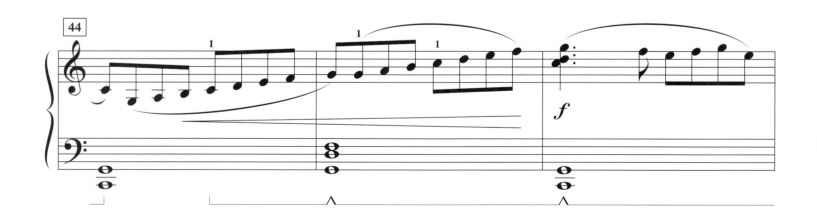

The Coventry Carol

Words attributed to Robert Croo   Ancient English Carol
arr. Timothy Brown

Gently, like a lullaby (♩ = ca. 126)

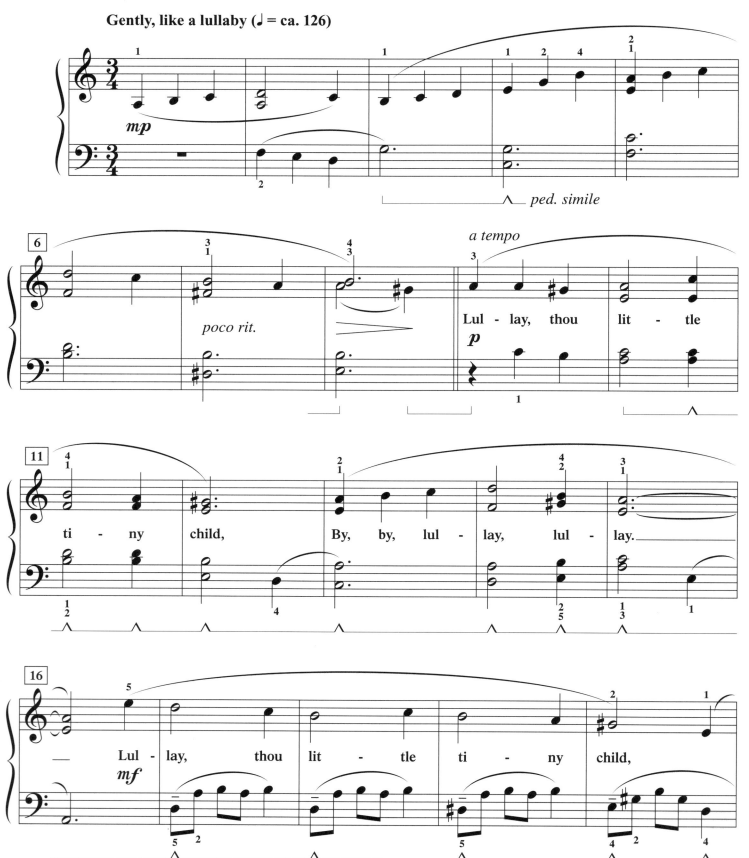

FJH1576

Silent Night
(Stille Nacht)

Franz Gruber   arr. Robert Schultz

Gently (♩ = 112)

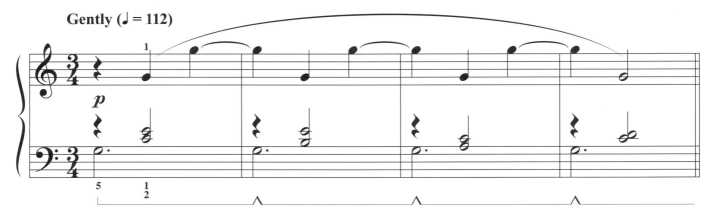

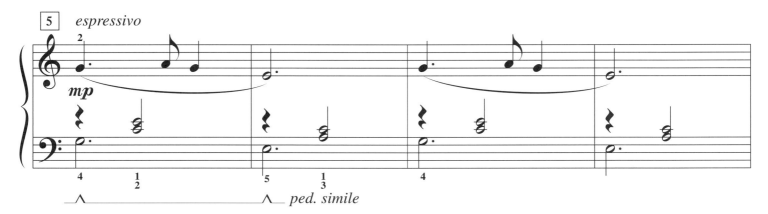

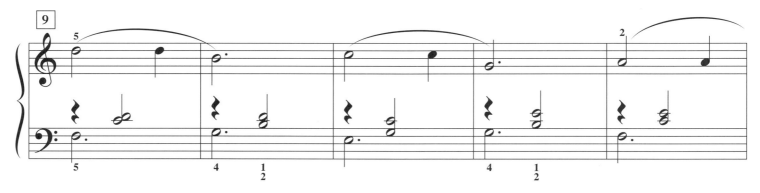

Teacher Accompaniment: (*Student plays one octave higher*)

FJH1576

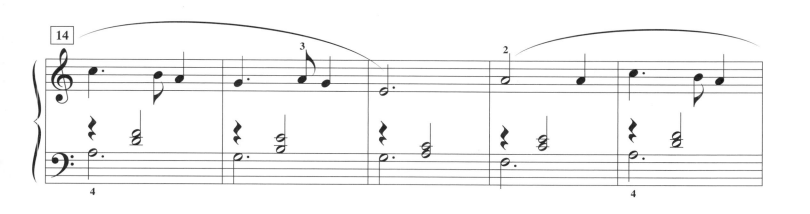

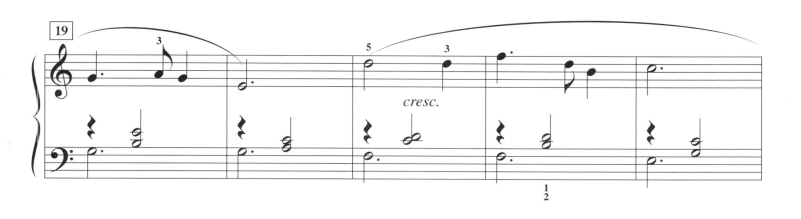

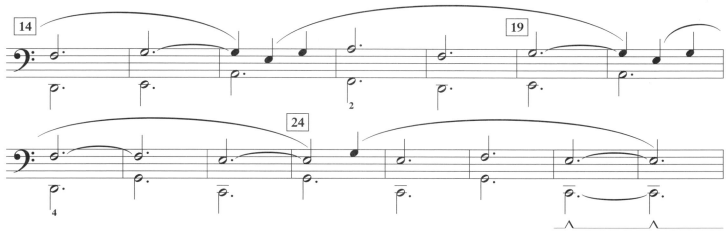

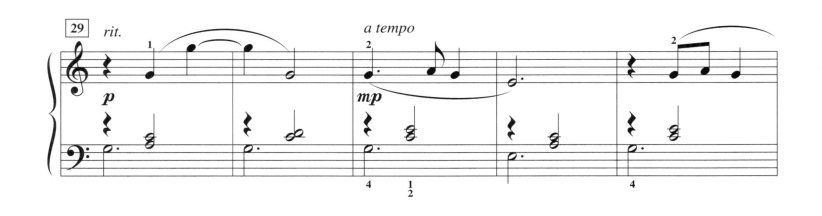

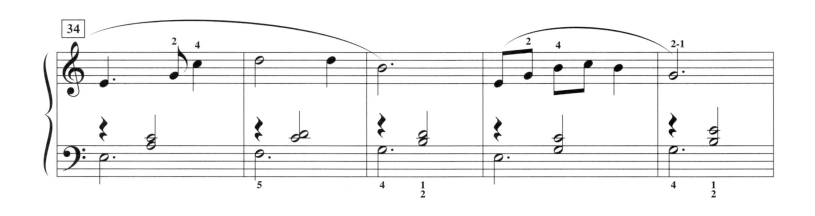

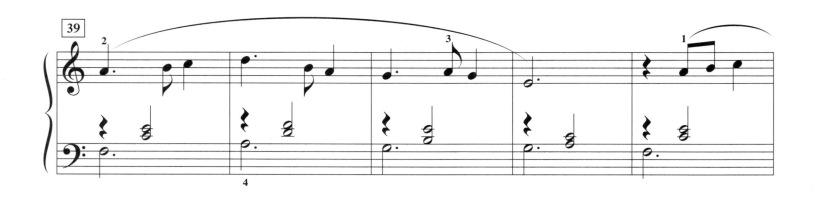

FJH1576

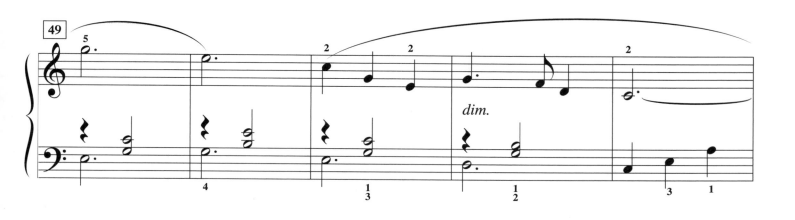

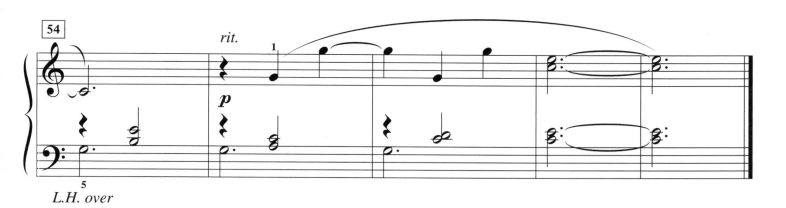

L.H. over

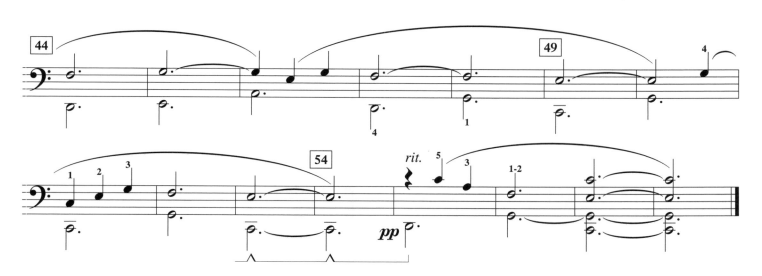

O Come, All Ye Faithful

(Adeste Fideles)

John Francis Wade   arr. Edwin McLean

With energy (♩ = 126-132)

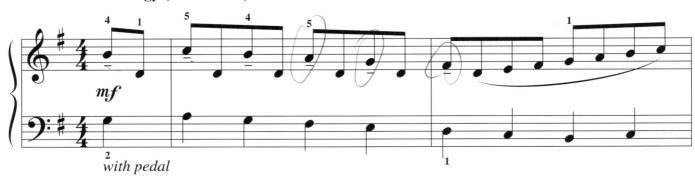

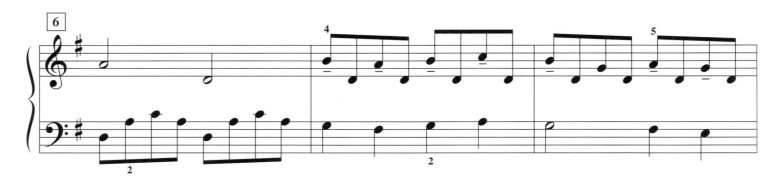

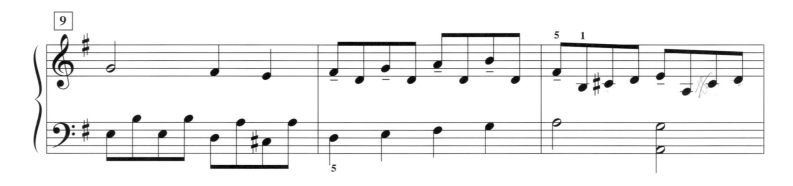

FJH1576

The First Nowell
(The First Noël)

Secondo

Traditional English Carol　　arr. Timothy Brown

FJH1576

The First Nowell

(The First Noël)

Primo

Traditional English Carol   arr. Timothy Brown

Andante (♩ = 92)

Secondo

Primo

Christmas Travels

Il est né: Old French Carol   *Gesu Bambino*: Pietro Alessandro Yon
O Tannenbaum: German Folk Song   arr. Kevin Olson

Il est né (France)

Calmly (♩ = 108)

con pedale

FJH1576

Gesu Bambino (Italy)

O Tannenbaum (Germany)

Tempo I

What Child Is This

(Greensleeves)

English Folk Song   arr. Melody Bober

FJH1576

Hallelujah Chorus
from *The Messiah*

George Frideric Handel   arr. Edwin McLean

Allegro (♩ = ca. 108)

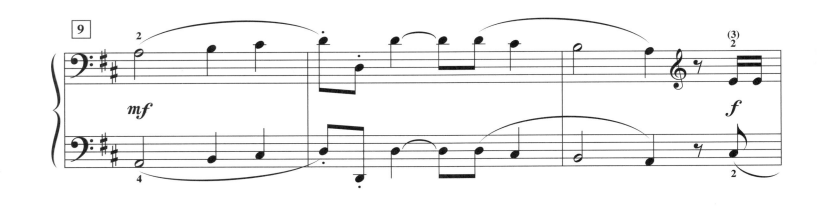

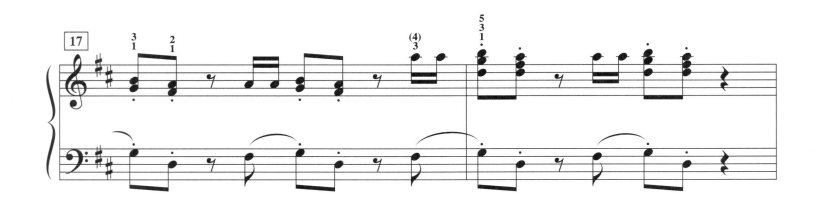

FJH1576

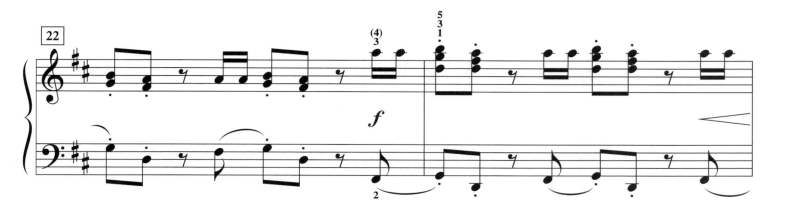

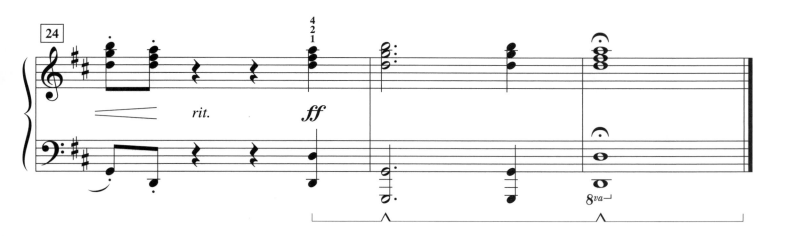

O Come, All Ye Faithful (*Adeste Fideles*)

Five hundred years ago, a Roman Catholic College for Englishmen was established in Douai, France. Nearly 300 years ago, this college produced one of the greatest of all Christmas carols, *Adeste Fideles*. John Francis Wade, a Catholic Englishman living there, created the Latin words and the music between the years of 1740 and 1743. In 1841 Frederick Oakeley began the English translation, which was published in London in 1852. This Christmas carol is among the most popular carols of the world.

The First Nowell (*The First Noël*)

Noël is an old French word meaning Christmas. Although the title suggests that this song comes from France, the words and music to this carol were probably created in Cornwall, England 500 years ago. The lyrics were published in 1823 and the music in 1833. This is one of the best-known carols of completely English origin, even though the word Noël is French!

Christmas Travels

Il est né

This is a traditional French carol. The music is of folk origin and was created about 300 years ago, and the lyrics may have been written around the same time. The tune comes from the air *La Tête bizarde*, an old Normandy hunting song. The text was first published in Dom G. Legeay's *Noêls anciens* (1875-1876).

Gesu Bambino

This Christmas classic, created by Pietro Alessandro Yon, has become a holiday favorite the world over. Pietro Yon was of Italian birth. He took his musical studies at Milan and Turin. He served as deputy organist at the Vatican in Rome, and was appointed honorary organist of the Basilica. He composed *Gesu Bambino*, his best-known piece, in 1917 in New York City, which eventually became his permanent home. The original lyrics were in both Italian and English, with the English written by Frederick Herman Martens.

FJH1570

O Christmas Tree (*O Tannenbaum*)

This popular German carol in honor of the fir tree is of folk origin, dating back 500 years. The custom of decorating trees for Christmas came about hundreds of years ago in the German Rhineland. By 1605 trees glittering with decorations were common; candles were added later in the century. Decorating trees was popularized in England by Queen Victoria's husband, Prince Albert, in 1841—the same year the decorations appeared on trees in Paris. The first American Christmas tree appeared in Pennsylvania in the 1830s.

What Child Is This

This carol uses the tune from the well-known English folk song titled *Greensleeves*. This folk song, composed 500 years ago, was an English air that was so popular that William Shakespeare mentioned it in *The Merry Wives of Windsor*. The lyrics for *What Child Is This* were written by the Englishman William Chatterton Dix around 1865. It is not known exactly when the lyrics and the music were paired, but they are now an important part of the Christmas holiday season.

Hallelujah Chorus

George Frideric Handel composed the entire *Messiah* oratorio, of which this chorus is a part, in twenty-four days, between August 22 and September 14, 1741. The *Hallelujah Chorus* is the most famous movement of the oratorio and is often sung at Christmas. In the United States, "Do It Yourself Messiahs" have become popular, giving people a chance to buy tickets to an orchestral concert and join in the singing of some selections, among them the *Hallelujah Chorus*. Perhaps you will invite people to sing when you play it!

ABOUT THE ARRANGERS

Melody Bober

Piano instructor, music teacher, composer, clinician—Melody Bober has been active in music education for over 25 years. As a composer, her goal is to create exciting and challenging pieces that are strong teaching tools to promote a lifelong love, understanding, and appreciation for music. Pedagogy, ear training, and musical expression are fundamentals of Melody's teaching, as well as fostering composition skills in her students.

Melody graduated with highest honors from the University of Illinois with a degree in music education, and later received a master's degree in piano performance. She maintains a large private studio, performs in numerous regional events, and conducts workshops across the country. She and her husband Jeff reside in Minnesota.

Timothy Brown

Timothy Brown did his undergraduate studies at Bowling Green State University and received his master's degree in piano performance from the University of North Texas. His past teachers include Adam Wodnicki, Newel Kay Brown and Robert Xavier Rodriguez. He was a recipient of a research fellowship from Royal Holloway, University of London, where he performed his postgraduate studies in music composition and orchestration with the English composer, Brian Lock. He later continued his research at the well known Accademia Nazionale di Santa Cecilia in Rome, Italy.

His numerous credits as a composer include the first prize at the Aliénor International Harpsichord Competition for his harpsichord solo *Suite Española* (Centaur records). His recent programs include his original compositions showcased at the Spoleto Music Festival, and the Library of Congress Concert Series in Washington D.C. His recent commissions and performances include world premieres by the Chapman University Chamber Orchestra and Concert Choir, the Carter Albrecht Music Foundation, the Rodgers Center for Holocaust Education, and the Daniel Pearl Music Foundation.

Timothy Brown is an exclusive composer/clinician for The FJH Music Company Inc. (ASCAP)

Kevin Costley

Kevin Costley holds several graduate degrees in the areas of elementary education and piano pedagogy, and literature, including a doctorate from Kansas State University. For nearly two decades, he was owner and director of The Keyboard Academy, specializing in innovative small group instruction. Kevin served for several years as head of the music department and on the keyboard faculty of Messenger College in Joplin, Missouri.

Kevin is a standing faculty member of Inspiration Point Fine Arts Colony piano and string camp, where he performs and teaches private piano, ensemble classes, and composition. He conducts child development seminars, writes for national publications, serves as a clinician for piano workshops, and adjudicates numerous piano festivals and competitions. Presently, Dr. Costley is an associate professor of early childhood education at Arkansas Tech University in Russellville, Arkansas.

FJH1576

Edwin McLean

Edwin McLean is a composer living in Chapel Hill, North Carolina. He is a graduate of the Yale School of Music, where he studied with Krzysztof Penderecki and Jacob Druckman. He also holds a master's degree in music theory and a bachelor's degree in piano performance from the University of Colorado.

Mr. McLean has authored over 200 publications for The FJH Music Company, ranging from *The FJH Classic Music Dictionary* to original works for pianists from beginner to advanced. His highly-acclaimed works for harpsichord have been performed internationally and are available on the Miami Bach Society recording, *Edwin McLean: Sonatas for 1, 2, and 3 Harpsichords*. His 2011 solo jazz piano album *Don't Say Goodbye* (CD1043) includes many of his advanced works for piano published by FJH.

Edwin McLean began his career as a professional arranger. Currently, he is senior editor for The FJH Music Company Inc.

Kevin Olson

Kevin Olson is an active pianist, composer, and member of the piano faculty at Utah State University, where he has taught a variety of courses, including piano literature, pedagogy, and accompanying. In addition to his collegiate teaching responsibilities, Kevin is a faculty advisor for the Utah State University Youth Conservatory, which provides weekly group and private piano instruction to more than 200 pre-college community students. The National Association of Schools of Music has recently recognized the Conservatory as a model for pre-college piano instruction programs. Before teaching at Utah State, he was on the faculty at Elmhurst College near Chicago and Humboldt State University in northern California.

A native of Utah, Kevin began composing at age five. When he was twelve, his composition, *An American Trainride*, received the Overall First Prize at the 1983 National PTA Convention at Albuquerque, New Mexico. Since then he has been a Composer in Residence at the National Conference on Keyboard Pedagogy, and has written music commissioned and performed by groups such as the American Piano Quartet, the American Festival Chorus and Orchestra, Chicago a cappella, the Rich Matteson Jazz Festival, Music Teachers National Association, and several piano teacher associations around the country.

Kevin maintains a large piano studio, teaching students of a variety of ages and abilities. Many of the needs of his own piano students have inspired more than 100 books and solos published by the FJH Music Company, which he joined as a writer in 1994.

Robert Schultz

Robert Schultz, composer, arranger, and editor, has achieved international fame during his career in the music publishing industry. The Schultz Piano Library, established in 1980, has included more than 500 publications of classical works, popular arrangements, and Schultz's original compositions in editions for pianists of every level from the beginner through the concert artist. In addition to his extensive library of published piano works, Schultz's output includes original orchestral works, chamber music, works for solo instruments, and vocal music.

Schultz has presented his published editions at workshops, clinics, and convention showcases throughout the United States and Canada. He is a long-standing member of ASCAP and has served as president of the Miami Music Teachers Association. Mr. Schultz's original piano compositions and transcriptions are featured on the compact disc recordings *Visions of Dunbar* and *Tina Faigen Plays Piano Transcriptions*, released on the ACA Digital label and available worldwide. His published original works for concert artists are noted in Maurice Hinson's *Guide to the Pianist's Repertoire, Third Edition*. He currently devotes his full time to composing and arranging. In-depth information about Robert Schultz and The Schultz Piano Library is available at the Website www.schultzmusic.com.

A great way to prepare for your Christmas recitals is to use the recordings in the following ways:

1) The first 12 tracks are the solo piano performances of each Christmas carol. Enjoy listening to these pieces anywhere anytime! Listen to them casually (as background music) and attentively. Follow along with your score as you listen and after you have finished listening, you might discuss interpretation with your teacher.

2) The rest of the tracks are to help you prepare for your Christmas recitals. The recordings can be used as a practice partner, because you can play along with the tracks! This is how it works: Each carol has two accompaniment tracks. The first accompaniment track is for practice. It is at a slower tempo so that you can learn to play with the accompaniment. You will hear your part along with the accompaniment. You can play hands separately or hands together. The second version of the accompaniment is the "performance-ready" track. It is *a tempo* and does not include your part. All it needs to make it complete is your piano playing!

In both versions, before the accompaniment begins, you will hear a steady beat for two measures so that you know the tempo.

All of the orchestrations were created by Dr. Kevin Olson on a Roland KR-7 piano.

FJH1576